D1358795

DATE DUE

CONTINENTS

Africa

Michael and Jane Pelusey

CHELSEA HOUSE
PUBLISHERS

A Haights Cross Communications Company

Philadelphia

This edition first published in 2005 in the United States of America by Chelsea House Publishers, a subsidiary of Haights Cross Communications.

Chelsea House Publishers
2080 Cabot Blvd West, Suite 201
Langhorne, PA 19047-1813

The Chelsea House world wide web address is www.chelseahouse.com

First published in 2004 by
MACMILLAN EDUCATION AUSTRALIA PTY LTD
627 Chapel Street, South Yarra 3141

Visit our website at www.macmillan.com.au

Associated companies and representatives throughout the world.

Copyright © Michael and Jane Pelusey 2004

Library of Congress Cataloging-in-Publication Data
    Pelusey, Michael.
    Africa / by Michael and Jane Pelusey.
    p. cm. – (Continents)
    Includes bibliographical references and index.
    ISBN 0-7910-8281-4
    1. Africa – Juvenile literature. 2. Africa – Geography – Juvenile literature. I. Pelusey, Jane. II. Title.
    DT3.P35 2004
    916'.02–dc22

                                                          2004015814

Edited by Angelique Campbell-Muir
Text design by Karen Young
Cover design by Karen Young
Illustrations by Nina Sanadze
Maps by Laurie Whiddon, Map Illustrations

Printed in China

Acknowledgements

The authors and the publisher are grateful to the following for permission to reproduce copyright material:

Cover photographs: Namib Desert, courtesy of Digital Vision. Zebras, courtesy of Photodisc.

AAP Image/AP PHOTO/RAOUF, p. 29; Australian Picture Library/Corbis, pp. 7, 17 (top), 21 (bottom); Corel, p. 11 (top); Digital Vision, p. 27 (bottom); Dr. Stuart Miller/Lochman Transparencies, pp. 3 (center), 9; Photodisc, pp. 10, 14 (bottom), 20 (left), 21 (top), 26, 27 (top); Photolibrary.com, pp. 11 (bottom), 14 (top); Photolibrary.com/Animals Animals, pp. 8 (top), 13 (top and bottom), 30; Photolibrary.com/Index Stock, pp. 3 (top), 16, 18 (bottom), 23 (top), 25 (top and bottom); Photolibrary.com/OSF, p. 23 (bottom); Photolibrary.com/Photo Researchers Inc., p. 15; Reuters, pp. 3 (bottom), 17 (bottom), 19, 28 (top and bottom); Stockbyte, p. 20 (right).

While every care has been taken to trace and acknowledge copyright, the publisher tenders their apologies for any accidental infringement where copyright has proved untraceable. Where the attempt has been unsuccessful, the publisher welcomes information that would redress the situation.

Please note

At the time of printing, the Internet addresses appearing in this book were correct. Owing to the dynamic nature of the Internet, however, we cannot guarantee that all these addresses will remain correct.

Contents

Glossary words

When a word is printed in **bold**, you can look up its meaning in the Glossary on page 31.

Africa is a continent

Africa is the second largest continent in the world. Look at a world map or a globe and you can see that the world is made up of water and land. The big areas of land are called continents. There are seven continents:

- Africa
- Antarctica
- Asia
- Australia
- Europe
- North America
- South America.

Borders

Borders of continents follow natural physical features such as coastlines and mountain ranges. Africa is almost completely surrounded by oceans, except where it joins Asia in Egypt. The Suez Canal was built near this border through Egypt to join the Mediterranean and Red seas.

Africa's sea borders are the:

- Atlantic Ocean
- Indian Ocean
- Mediterranean Sea
- Red Sea.

World map showing the seven modern-day continents

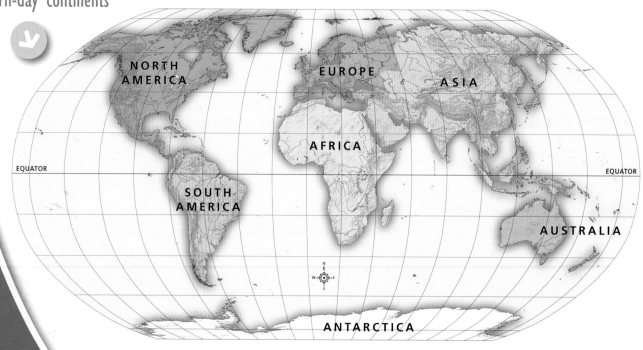

NORTH AMERICA

EUROPE

ASIA

AFRICA

EQUATOR

SOUTH AMERICA

AUSTRALIA

ANTARCTICA

The world is a jigsaw

The Earth's crust is made up of huge plates, called **tectonic plates**, which fit together like a jigsaw puzzle. These plates are constantly moving, up and down and sideways, up to 4 inches (10 centimeters) a year. Over long periods of time, the plates change in size and shape as their edges push against each other.

Around 250 million years ago, there was one massive supercontinent called Pangaea. Around 200 million years ago, it began splitting and formed two continents. Laurasia was the northern continent and Gondwana was the southern continent. By about 65 million years ago, Laurasia and Gondwana had separated into smaller landmasses that look much like the continents we know today. Laurasia split to form Europe, Asia, and North America. Gondwana split to form South America, Africa, Australia, and Antarctica.

Africa was once part of the supercontinent Pangaea.

The African continent formed when Gondwana split into smaller landmasses.

Early Africa

When the continents were one, animals moved across the land, since there was no water to stop them. When the continents split apart, the animals were left on separate landmasses and they began to change and develop into the animals we know today. During this time, dinosaurs roamed the Earth, including Africa. In fact, the bones of a 90-foot-(27-meter-) long plant-eating dinosaur called the Barosaurus were found in Tanzania. As the dinosaurs became **extinct**, other animals took over. **Mammals** developed over millions of years. They were the distant ancestors of the antelopes, elephants, zebras, and giraffes we see in Africa today.

What's in a word?
The word *Africa* is not an African word. In the old Latin language, *Africa* means "sunny." In Greek, *Aphrike* means "not cold." Africa is both sunny and not cold, so this is probably where the name came from.

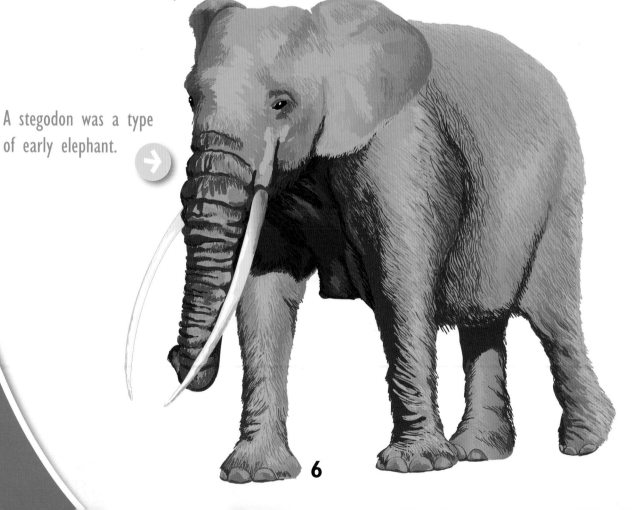

A stegodon was a type of early elephant.

Early humans

Scientists believe modern humans, or *Homo sapiens*, came from Africa. In 1997, the bones of the earliest type of *Homo sapiens* were found in Africa. They are thought to be 160,000 years old. Scientists believe early humans moved from Africa and spread around the world.

First civilizations

The early African humans hunted animals and gathered fruits and berries for food. When their food ran out they moved to find more. About 10,000 years ago, humans discovered that they could grow some plants or crops and keep animals for food. Humans then had no need to move around to find food. They settled in a place and built towns. The towns grew into cities and civilizations began.

Archaeologists working at a dig site in Egypt in 2001

A great African civilization

Egypt had one of the world's great civilizations. The first **pharaoh** was King Narmer who ruled Egypt 5,000 years ago. The Egyptian pharaohs built the pyramids to be their tombs when they died. The last pharaoh was Queen Cleopatra VII. She died in 30 B.C., more than 2,000 years ago.

Africa today

The Seychelles Islands are surrounded by beautiful coral reefs.

The physical features of the African continent

Africa is the second largest continent after Asia, covering about one-fifth of the total land surface of the Earth. It covers an area of 11.7 million square miles (30.3 million square kilometers). It is made up of 53 countries, including six islands: São Tomé and Príncipe, Madagascar, Comoros, Mauritius, Seychelles, and Cape Verde.

The biggest country in Africa is Sudan, with an area of 967,500 square miles (2,505,818 square kilometers). The smallest African country is the Seychelles Islands, with an area of 104 square miles (270 square kilometers).

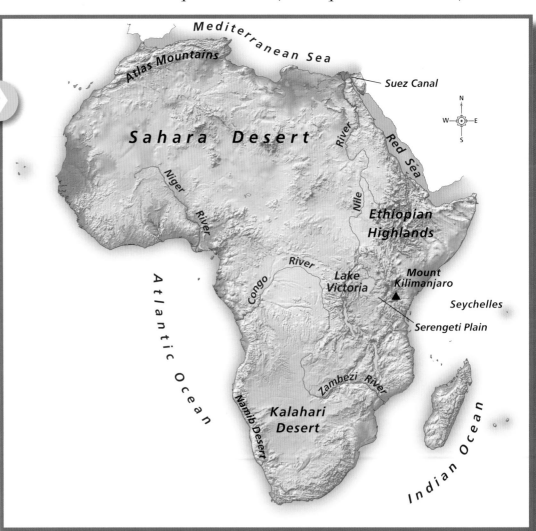

Physical features

Africa's land lies north and south of the **equator**. The northern part of Africa is desert, made up of dry rocky land and sand dunes. South of the deserts are plains. These are big flat areas of land covered in grass and scrub called **savanna**. Low parts of the plains fill up with water and become huge lakes. Rising from the plains to the east and south are mountain ranges and high flat plains called plateaus. Africa's rivers start in these **highlands** and flow through the plains to the sea. Near the equator, the continent becomes much wetter where **rain forests** grow. Like the north, parts of the south are also dry deserts.

People

The people of Africa have learned to live in harsh environments such as deserts and rain forests. Most Africans live in places where there is enough rainfall to grow crops. African people belong to different **ethnic groups**, or tribes, each with its own **traditions**.

Zebras drinking from a lake on the Serengeti Plain

The land

Africa's land is mostly deserts and plains.

Deserts

Africa has many huge deserts. The Sahara is the world's largest desert and covers an area of 3,500,000 square miles (9,065,000 square kilometers). Much of the Sahara Desert is so dry and rocky that people cannot grow crops for food. The Namib Desert in Namibia is dominated by huge sand dunes. The Kalahari Desert in southern Africa is covered in small prickly bushes.

Plains

The Serengeti in Tanzania and the Masai Mara in Kenya are both savanna plains. Big African animals, such as wildebeests, move over the plains in huge herds looking for fresh grass to eat. Tribes of people also graze cattle on Africa's plains.

The world's biggest desert

The Sahara Desert is the largest desert in the world. It is more than 3.5 million square miles (9 million square kilometers) in size. It is almost as big as the whole of the United States.

The Sahara Desert is partly covered by sand dunes.

Mountains

There are many mountain ranges in Africa. Africa's highest mountain is Kilimanjaro in Tanzania. It rises 19,341 feet (5,895 meters) above sea level. The Atlas Mountains in Morocco are also high. Small tribes of people live in these **barren** mountains. They keep goats and sheep for food. The highlands in Ethiopia are very rugged with some peaks more than 9,000 feet (3,000 meters) high.

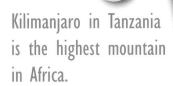

Kilimanjaro in Tanzania is the highest mountain in Africa.

Rivers

Rivers are important to the African people for transportation, water, and fishing. The major rivers in Africa are the Nile, the Congo, the Niger, and the Zambezi.

Lakes

The largest lake in Africa is Lake Victoria in Uganda, Tanzania, and Kenya. It covers an area of 26,828 square miles (69,484 square kilometers).

The world's longest river

The Nile River is the longest river in the world. It is 4,160 miles (6,695 kilometers) long. It flows from Lake Victoria to the Mediterranean Sea in Egypt.

A village on the Nile River near Aswan in Egypt

The climate

Africa is a big continent, so it has many climates. The main climates in Africa are **arid**, savanna, and **tropical**.

Arid and semiarid

African deserts have an arid climate. They are hot and dry. In 1922, a part of the Sahara Desert in Libya recorded the highest temperature in the world when it climbed to 136 degrees Fahrenheit (58 degrees Celsius). Areas near the edges of deserts receive a little more rain and have a semiarid climate. People can grow some crops in these areas.

Climate zones in Africa →

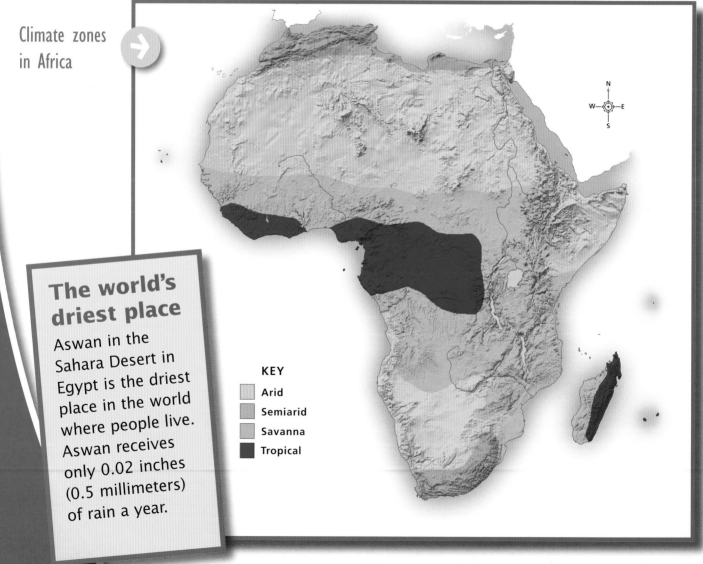

KEY

- Arid
- Semiarid
- Savanna
- Tropical

The world's driest place

Aswan in the Sahara Desert in Egypt is the driest place in the world where people live. Aswan receives only 0.02 inches (0.5 millimeters) of rain a year.

Wet season thunderstorms are common in the savanna.

The world's wettest places

Debundscha in Cameroon is one of the wettest places in the world. It gets 405 inches (10,290 millimeters) of rain every year. Monrovia, the capital of Liberia, is the second wettest place inhabited by people. Monrovia's yearly rainfall is 202 inches (5,131 millimeters).

Savanna

Africa's savanna has two seasons known as the hot wet and the hot dry. The wet season brings heavy rainfall while the rest of the year is dry.

Tropical

Near the equator, Africa has a tropical climate. Here it is hot and **humid** all the time. Heavy rain falls nearly every day. Lots of rain and heat make it perfect for rain forests to grow in this part of Africa. People grow tropical fruits and other crops that like hot and wet weather. Sometimes there is so much rain that rivers overflow, flooding villages and crops.

The Montane Rain Forest in Mantady National Park, Madagascar, is an example of a tropical rain forest.

Thunder and lightning

Thunder and lightning occur with tropical storms. A town in Uganda called Tororo holds the record for the most thunderstorm days in a single year. Imagine 251 days of thunder and lightning every year!

Plants and animals

Africa is the home of many plants and animals not found on other continents.

Baobab trees are able to survive in the savanna.

Savanna

Trees and grasses that grow in this area have learned to live in the sometimes dry and sometimes wet climate of the savanna. The baobab tree has a swollen trunk that stores water during the dry season.

The savanna region is home to huge herds of grazing animals such as wildebeests and zebras. Large members of the cat family, such as lions, cheetahs, and leopards, live on the grasslands where they catch and eat the grazing animals. Some of Africa's biggest animals, such as the African elephant, hippopotamus, rhinoceros, and giraffe, also roam these grasslands.

The world's fastest animal

The cheetah can run at 68 miles (110 kilometers) per hour. The cheetah needs to run fast to catch its favorite food, the Thomson's gazelle. The gazelle can run at 59 miles (95 kilometers) per hour.

A cheetah's body is designed for running fast.

A wild female mountain gorilla in Bwindi Impenetrable Forest National Park, Uganda

Tropical rain forest

Tall trees grow in the tropical rain forest. Smaller plants such as ferns and palms grow in the shade under the trees.

Two of the great apes, chimpanzees and gorillas, live in the tropical rain forests. They eat fruit, seeds, and leaves from the tropical plants.

Desert

Desert animals have adapted to living without water, with high temperatures and food shortages for long periods. The small mice and rats that live in the deserts eat seeds and leaves that contain tiny amounts of water. Camels can store water and survive for up to two weeks without drinking. Desert plants tend to have small leaves to reduce water loss in the dry conditions.

Animals at risk

For different reasons, some African animals are **endangered**:

- The Black rhinoceros is hunted for its horn, which is used for a medicine
- Elephants are hunted for their ivory tusks
- Leopards are hunted for their fur coats
- Crocodiles are hunted and skinned to make shoes and bags
- The gorilla is also rare because the forest where it lives is being cut down for timber and farmland.

The people

Africa is home to thousands of ethnic groups or tribes. Each group has its own traditions, beliefs, and languages.

Ethnic groups

The people of North Africa are Berbers who came from the **Middle East**. Some Berbers, called Bedouins, are **nomads** who move from **oasis** to oasis throughout the Sahara Desert, herding goats and sheep. More than 1,500 different ethnic groups live south of the Sahara Desert. As well as some lifestyle differences, some tribes also look physically different from others. The Mbuti are short people less than 5 feet (150 centimeters) tall. They live in the rain forest of tropical Africa and are skillful hunters, using poison-tipped arrows to catch animals for food. The Zulus of South Africa are tall people, who stand up to and more than 6 feet (182 centimeters) tall. They keep cattle and grow crops.

People facts	
Population	807 million people
Most populated country	Nigeria with 117 million people
Least populated country	São Tomé and Príncipe with 153,000 people
Most crowded country	Mauritius with 1,671 people per square mile (645 people per square kilometer)

Zulu men dancing in traditional clothing

Languages

There are many languages spoken in Africa. Each tribe has its own language. Most tribes in the east speak Swahili. The Mbuti people speak Bantu, which is a common African language. The Berbers speak Arabic. Other languages such as French, English, and Dutch were introduced when people from Europe **colonized** Africa.

Religion

Many Northern Africans are Muslims and follow the **Islamic** religion, which originally came from the Middle East. Many African tribes have their own traditional beliefs. They believe in gods that represent physical features such as nearby mountains or rivers.

Culture

Each tribe in Africa has its own forms of dress. The Wodaabe men of West Africa paint their faces to show their beauty. Once a year the men stand in a line while Wodaabe women choose their husbands-to-be. The Masai people of Kenya wear large circles of beads around their necks and in their earlobes.

The Mosque in Mopti, Mali, was built in 1935 and is made of mud.

Masai people in traditional clothing

The countries

The 53 countries that make up Africa can be divided into four regions:

- Northern Africa
- semiarid Africa
- tropical Africa
- Southern Africa.

These regions are based on climate, location, and ethnic groups.

The African countries we know today did not exist 300 years ago, as the land belonged to many different African tribes. The borders within Africa today are those made by European people.

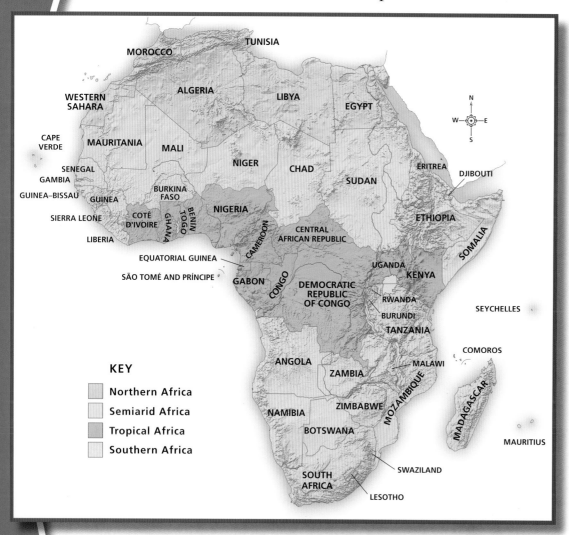

KEY

- Northern Africa
- Semiarid Africa
- Tropical Africa
- Southern Africa

European colonies

About 500 years ago, people from Great Britain, Portugal, the Netherlands, Spain, and France started coming to Africa. They began **trading** with Africans for gold and ivory. Trading with Africa became so valuable that, by the 1800s, nearly all of Africa belonged to or became colonies of European countries. European colonists brought with them languages such as English and French, and taught Africans about the **Christian** religion.

South African cricket fans enjoy a World Cup match in Johannesburg in 2003, without **segregation**.

African tribal groups

The Europeans who came to Africa did not recognize the different African tribal groups. When they divided the continent into separate countries, some friendly tribes were divided by a border while warring tribes were grouped together in one country.

Many Africans resisted European rule and started fighting for their own **independence**. From the 1950s, African countries began to win their independence from Europe. Without European rule, some old tribal enemies began fighting again. There is still fighting between tribes in Sudan and the Congo.

Afrikaners

During the colonial time, South Africa was part of Great Britain. Farmers from the Netherlands also settled in South Africa. Fighting broke out when they farmed land that once belonged to African tribes. The Dutch were better armed and won these battles even though they were outnumbered. In 1948, the Dutch settlers, known as Afrikaners, took over South Africa from the British. They ruled South Africa under **apartheid**, a system that separated white and black people. Black Africans were banned from white areas. Apartheid was officially abandoned in South Africa in 1994.

There are six countries in Northern Africa. Use the key below to find out about and compare each country's languages, religions, ethnic groups, agriculture, and natural resources.

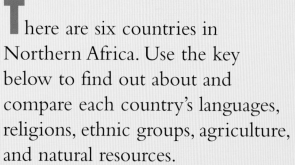

Countries	Languages	Religions	Ethnic groups	Agriculture	Natural resources
Algeria	■ ■ ■	☪ ✡	🧍	✤ ✺ ⬤ ☆	◆ ◆ ◆ ◆ ◆
Egypt	■ ■ ■ ■	☪ ✝ ✡	🧍 🧍	◎ ✤ ✤ ☆	◆ ◆ ◆ ◆ ◆
Libya	■ ■ ■	☪	✤ ✦ ⬤ ☆ ✺	◆
Morocco	■ ■ ■	☪ ✡	🧍	✤ ✺ ⬤ ☆ ✤	◆ ◆ ◆ ◆ ◆
Tunisia	■ ■	☪ ✡	🧍	✤ ✺ ⬤ ☆ ✦ ✤	◆ ◆ ◆ ◆ ◆
Western Sahara (partly occupied by Morocco)	■ ■ ■	☪ ✡	🧍	☆ ✤	◆ ◆

Key	Languages	Religions	Ethnic groups	Agriculture	Natural resources
	■ Arabic ■ Berber ■ English ■ Ethnic languages ■ French ■ Italian ■ Spanish	✝ Christianity ☪ Islam ✡ Judaism	🧍 Arab-Berber 🧍 Egyptian 🧍 European	✤ Cereal grains ✺ Citrus ◎ Cotton ✦ Dates ✤ Fruit and vegetables ⬤ Olives ☆ Sheep, cattle, and goats	◆ Iron ore ◆ Lead ◆ Oil and gas ◆ Phosphates ◆ Salt ◆ Zinc

Official name: Arab Republic of Egypt

Area: 386,660 square miles
(1,001,450 square kilometers)

Population: 68 million

Capital: Cairo

Major cities: Alexandria, Port Said

Colonial rule: Ottoman (1250–1800), France
(early 1800s), England (late 1800s–early 1900s)

Famous landmarks: Pyramids of Giza,
Valley of the Kings, Sphinx

Famous people: Omar Sharif (actor),
King Farouk of Egypt

Traditions: belly dancing, hieroglyphs (an early form of writing),
mummification (to preserve dead bodies)

Traditional food: bab ghanoush (mashed eggplant), hummus
(chickpea and garlic dip)

Cairo, on the Nile River, has
the second largest population
of all the cities in Africa.

The Nile River flows through Egypt. The land near the Nile River is very
fertile. It is believed that the banks of the Nile were one of the first places in
the world where food crops were grown. The rest of Egypt is desert.

Morocco in focus

Official name: Kingdom of Morocco

Area: 172,413 square miles
(446,550 square kilometers)

Population: 30 million

Capital: Rabat

Major cities: Casablanca, Fez, Marrakech

Colonial rule: France, Spain

Famous landmarks: Djemaa El Fna Market in
Marrakech, Atlas Mountains

Famous people: King Hassan II (ruled Morocco
from 1961–1999)

Traditions: carpet making

Traditional food: dates; couscous (a small pasta made from flour
and water); lamb with spices such as cinnamon, cumin, coriander,
saffron, paprika, and ginger; sweet mint tea

A Berber herder with his goat
herd in the Atlas Mountains

Morocco is only 8 miles (12 kilometers) from Europe. The Sahara Desert
and the Atlas Mountains are the main land features in Morocco.

Semiarid Africa

There are 15 countries in semiarid Africa. Use the key below to find out about and compare each country's languages, religions, ethnic groups, agriculture, and natural resources.

Countries	Languages	Religions	Ethnic groups	Agriculture	Natural resources
Burkina Faso					
Chad					
Djibouti					
Eritrea					
Ethiopia					
Gambia					
Guinea					
Guinea Bissau					
Mali					
Mauritania					
Niger					
Senegal					
Sierra Leone					
Somalia					
Sudan					

Key

Languages	Religions	Ethnic groups	Agriculture	Natural resources
Arabic	Christianity	Arab	Cereal grains	Coal
English	Islam	Different African tribes	Coffee	Copper
Ethnic languages	Traditional beliefs	European	Cotton	Diamonds
French			Dates	Gold
Italian			Fruit and vegetables	**Hydropower**
Portuguese			Peanuts	Iron ore
			Sheep, cattle, and goats	Lead
			Sugar	Oil and gas
				Phosphates
				Salt
				Silver
				Timber
				Tin
				Uranium
				Zinc

Ethiopia in focus

Official name: Federal Democratic Republic of Ethiopia

Area: 435,184 square miles (1,127,127 square kilometers)

Population: 69 million

Capital: Addis Ababa

Major cities: Dire Dawa, Jima

Colonial rule: none

Famous landmarks: Lalibela (800-year-old Christian church), Sof Omar Caves (significant to Muslim people)

Famous people: Haile Gebrselassie (Olympic gold medalist and world champion runner), Abebe Biki (Olympic gold medalist marathon runner)

Traditions: Christianity came to Ethiopia 1,700 years ago

Traditional food: injera (bread made from an Ethiopian grain called teff), coffee (believed to have originated in Ethiopia)

Ethiopia is mostly a mountainous country with semiarid plains in between the mountains. The country sometimes suffers long droughts with many people dying of starvation. It is the only African country never to have been colonized.

Lalibela is carved from rock.

Senegal in focus

Official name: Republic of Senegal

Area: 75,749 square miles (196,190 square kilometers)

Population: 10 million

Capital: Dakar

Major cities: Thies, Pikine

Colonial rule: France

Famous landmarks: Lake Guier, Senegal River

Famous people: Youssou N'Dour and Touré Kunda (world-famous musicians who combine traditional music with pop music)

Traditions: Senegalese music

Traditional food: stew with peanuts, rice cooked in a fish and vegetable sauce

Senegal is mostly a flat land with savanna grasslands. Peanut crops are the most important crop grown in Senegal. This is because the climate and soils of Senegal are just right for growing peanuts.

Senegalese people use nets to catch fish along the beaches.

Tropical Africa

There are 16 countries in tropical Africa. Use the key below to find out about and compare each country's languages, religions, ethnic groups, agriculture, and natural resources.

Countries	Languages	Religions	Ethnic groups	Agriculture	Natural resources
Benin	English, Ethnic languages	Traditional beliefs, Christianity, Islam	Different African tribes	Cereal grains, Cotton, Fruit and vegetables, Peanuts, Sheep/cattle/goats, Cocoa	Oil and gas, Copper
Burundi	English, Ethnic languages	Christianity, Traditional beliefs, Islam	Different African tribes	Coffee, Cotton, Tea, Fruit and vegetables, Peanuts, Sheep/cattle/goats, Cocoa	Copper, Copper, Copper
Cameroon	English, Ethnic languages, French	Traditional beliefs, Christianity, Islam	Different African tribes, European	Coffee, Cotton, Tea, Fruit and vegetables, Sheep/cattle/goats, Cocoa	Oil and gas, Iron ore, Copper, Copper
Central African Republic	English, Ethnic languages	Traditional beliefs, Christianity, Islam	Different African tribes	Cotton, Coffee, Tea	Copper, Copper, Oil and gas, Iron ore, Copper
Congo	English, Ethnic languages	Christianity, Traditional beliefs	Different African tribes	Sugar, Fruit and vegetables, Peanuts, Coffee, Cocoa	Oil and gas, Copper, Copper, Copper, Copper, Copper
Cotê d'Ivoire	English, Ethnic languages	Christianity, Islam, Traditional beliefs	Different African tribes, European	Coffee, Cocoa, Fruit and vegetables, Sugar, Cotton	Oil and gas, Copper, Iron ore, Copper, Copper
Democratic Republic of Congo	English, Ethnic languages	Christianity, Islam	Different African tribes	Coffee, Sugar, Tea, Fruit and vegetables	Copper, Copper, Iron ore, Copper, Copper, Copper
Equatorial Guinea	Spanish, Ethnic languages, English	Christianity, Traditional beliefs	Different African tribes	Coffee, Cocoa, Fruit and vegetables, Peanuts, Sheep/cattle/goats	Oil and gas, Copper, Copper
Gabon	English, Ethnic languages	Christianity, Traditional beliefs	Different African tribes, European	Cocoa, Coffee, Sugar, Sheep/cattle/goats	Oil and gas, Copper, Copper, Iron ore, Copper
Ghana	English, Ethnic languages	Traditional beliefs, Islam, Christianity	Different African tribes	Cocoa, Fruit and vegetables, Coffee, Peanuts	Copper, Copper, Copper
Kenya	English, Ethnic languages	Christianity, Traditional beliefs, Islam	Different African tribes	Coffee, Tea, Fruit and vegetables, Sugar, Sheep/cattle/goats	Copper, Iron ore
Liberia	English, Ethnic languages	Traditional beliefs, Christianity, Islam	Different African tribes	Coffee, Cocoa, Fruit and vegetables, Sugar, Sheep/cattle/goats	Iron ore, Copper, Copper, Copper
Nigeria	English, Ethnic languages	Islam, Christianity, Traditional beliefs	Different African tribes	Peanuts, Cotton, Cocoa, Fruit and vegetables, Sheep/cattle/goats	Oil and gas, Iron ore, Copper, Copper, Copper, Copper, Copper
Rwanda	English, Ethnic languages, French	Christianity, Islam	Different African tribes	Coffee, Tea, Fruit and vegetables, Sheep/cattle/goats	Copper, Copper, Copper
Togo	English, Ethnic languages	Traditional beliefs, Christianity, Islam	Different African tribes	Coffee, Cocoa, Cotton, Fruit and vegetables, Sheep/cattle/goats	Iron ore
Uganda	English, Ethnic languages	Christianity, Islam, Traditional beliefs	Different African tribes	Sugar, Coffee, Tea, Cotton, Fruit and vegetables, Sheep/cattle/goats	Copper, Copper, Copper

Key

Languages	Religions	Ethnic groups	Agriculture	Natural resources
■ English	✝ Christianity	Different African tribes	❖ Cereal grains	◆ Coal
■ Ethnic languages	☾ Islam	European	■ Cocoa	◆ Copper
■ French	☼ Traditional beliefs		✳ Coffee	◆ Diamonds
■ Spanish			◎ Cotton	◆ Gold
			❖ Fruit and vegetables	◆ Hydropower
			✳ Peanuts	◆ Iron ore
			☆ Sheep, cattle, and goats	◆ Lead
			▭ Sugar	● Oil and gas
			✿ Tea	◆ Phosphates
				◆ Salt
				◆ Silver
				◆ Timber
				◆ Tin
				◆ Uranium
				◆ Zinc

Ghana in focus

Official name: Republic of Ghana

Area: 92,100 square miles
(238,540 square kilometers)

Population: 19 million

Capital: Accra

Major cities: Tema, Cape Coast

Colonial rule: England

Famous landmarks: Lake Volta (world's largest man-made lake formed by a dam)

Famous people: Kofi Annan (United Nations leader)

Traditions: Ashanti tribe crafts (dolls)

Traditional food: soups and stews; root vegetables such as cassava, yam, or manioc that has been cooked and mashed into a ball

The fruit of the cocoa plant is used to make chocolate.

The northern part of Ghana is mainly savanna grasslands. In the southern part there is tropical rain forest. People in Ghana grow the cocoa plant.

Kenya in focus

Official name: Republic of Kenya

Area: 224,961 square miles
(582,650 square kilometers)

Population: 32 million

Capital: Nairobi

Major cities: Kisumu, Mombasa, Meru

Colonial rule: England

Famous landmarks: Masai Mara plain

Famous people: Richard Leakey (studied African animals and helped to save them from being hunted)

Traditions: safari

Traditional food: nyama choma
(barbecued meat)

Tourists visit safari parks, such as this one in the Masai Mara, Kenya, to see wild animals in their natural environment.

Most of Kenya is made up of high plateaus. Tea and coffee grow well on Kenya's plateaus because of the cool climate. Zebras, elephants, wildebeests, giraffes, antelopes, lions, and hyenas all live on the Kenyan plains.

Southern Africa

There are 11 countries in Southern Africa. Use the key below to find out about and compare each country's languages, religions, ethnic groups, agriculture, and natural resources.

Countries	Languages	Religions	Ethnic groups	Agriculture	Natural resources
Angola	■ ■	☼ ✝	🧍 🧍	☐ ❖ ✳ ◎ ☆	● ◆ ◆ ◆ ◆ ◆ ◆ ◆
Botswana	■	☼ ✝	🧍 🧍	☆ ❖	◆ ◆ ◆ ◆ ◆ ◆
Lesotho	■ ■	✝ ☼	🧍	❖ ☆	◆
Malawi	■ ■	✝ ☾	🧍	✿ ☐ ◎ ❖ ☆	◆ ◆ ◆
Mozambique	■ ■	☼ ✝ ☾	🧍	◎ ☐ ✿ ❖ ❖ ◎ ☆	◆ ● ◆
Namibia	■ ■ ■	✝ ☼	🧍 🧍	❖ ✳ ☆	◆ ◆ ◆ ◆ ◆ ◆ ◆ ● ◆
South Africa	■ ■ ■	✝ ☼	🧍 🧍	❖ ☐ ❖ ☆	◆ ◆ ◆ ◆ ◆ ◆ ◆ ●
Swaziland	■ ■	✝ ☼	🧍 🧍	☐ ◎ ❖ ◎ ❖ ✳ ☆	◆ ◆ ◆ ◆
Tanzania	■ ■ ■	✝ ☾ ☼	🧍	✳ ◎ ❖ ❖ ☆	◆ ◆ ◆ ◆ ◆ ◆ ● ◆ ◆
Zambia	■ ■	✝ ☾	🧍	❖ ✳ ❖ ◎ ☐ ☆ ✳	◆ ◆ ◆ ◆ ◆ ◆ ◆ ◆
Zimbabwe	■ ■	✝ ☼	🧍	❖ ◎ ✳ ☐ ❖ ☆	◆ ◆ ◆ ◆ ◆ ◆

Key	Languages	Religions	Ethnic groups	Agriculture	Natural resources
	■ Afrikaans ■ Arabic ■ English ■ Ethnic languages ■ Portuguese	✝ Christianity ☾ Islam ☼ Traditional beliefs	🧍 European 🧍 Various African tribes	❖ Cereal grains ◎ Citrus ✳ Coffee ◎ Cotton ❖ Fruit and vegetables ✳ Peanuts ☆ Sheep, cattle, and goats ☐ Sugar ✿ Tea	◆ Coal ◆ Copper ◆ Diamonds ◆ Gold ◆ Hydropower ◆ Iron ore ◆ Lead ● Oil and gas ◆ Phosphates ◆ Salt ◆ Silver ◆ Timber ◆ Tin ◆ Uranium ◆ Zinc

South Africa in focus

Official name: Republic of South Africa

Area: 471,008 square miles
(1,219,912 square kilometers)

Population: 46 million

Capital: Pretoria

Major cities: Cape Town, Johannesburg

Colonial rule: England, the Netherlands

Famous landmarks: Table Mountain,
Cape of Good Hope

Famous people: Nelson Mandela (fought against
apartheid and was arrested by the South African government,
spent 27 years in jail from 1962 to 1990, before becoming
South Africa's first black president in 1994 until 1999);
Ladysmith Black Mambazo (musical group)

Traditions: music (traditional and modern)

Traditional food: boerewors (sausage)

Table Mountain sits high
behind Cape Town.

South Africa is the richest country in Africa. It has a mild climate with good rainfall for
growing crops. South Africa is the world's biggest producer of gold and diamonds.

Namibia in focus

Official name: Republic of Namibia

Area: 317,872 square miles
(823,290 square kilometers)

Population: 1.7 million

Capital: Windhoek

Major cities: Keetmanshoop, Walvis Bay

Colonial rule: Germany

Famous landmarks: Skeleton Coast, Namib Desert

Famous people: Sam Nujoma (first president
in 1990)

Traditions: San people speak with clicking sounds

Traditional food: corn porridge eaten with fish,
goat, lamb, or beef and pumpkins, peppers, and onions

Giant red sand dunes are a
feature of the Namib Desert.

The Namib and Kalahari deserts cover most of the country. Tribal
people live in the dry country and keep goats and cattle for food.
Elephants, antelopes, and lions also survive in this harsh environment.

Africa's future

This 80-year-old woman is carrying her 5-year-old malnourished grandson past the carcasses of her dead cattle herd near Afder. She will walk 684 miles (1,100 kilometers) to Addis Ababa for help.

Africa has many problems that need to be fixed to make life better for its people. Disease, **famine**, racial inequality, and fighting between tribes kill many people every year. The African people and various humanitarian organizations are working to solve these problems.

Health

A disease called AIDS (acquired immunodeficiency syndrome) started in Africa and spread throughout the world. AIDS stops people's bodies from fighting infections and is killing thousands of Africans every year.

Famine

Parts of Africa such as Ethiopia and Sudan often experience droughts. Without rain, crops fail and livestock die. People starve from lack of food.

Crowded cities

To find work, many African people are leaving their farms and moving to the big cities. These cities are becoming very crowded. Nearly 12 million people live in Cairo. Lagos in Nigeria has 13 million people.

Lagos in Nigeria is the most crowded city in Africa.

28

This Sudanese volunteer is giving an oral **vaccine** to a child in Khartoum. This was part of a 1999 campaign to eradicate polio in Sudan by 2000.

Lending a helping hand

Charity organizations raise money to help African people who are sick or cannot afford good living conditions. They teach people better ways to dig wells to get clean drinking water from the ground and grow crops to produce more food. Organizations such as the Save the Children Fund and Red Cross use donations to fund schools, health, housing, and food projects in Africa. The Save the Children Fund is supplying food to thousands of children and their families in Malawi who are starving because their crops have failed after floods, which were followed by a drought.

Tourism

Many thousands of tourists come to Africa to see elephants, lions, giraffes, and other wild animals in huge game parks. Local people are employed as park wardens in these game parks. Tourists also bring their money into the country and spend it at local businesses such as hotels, restaurants, and souvenir stores.

Africa in review

Africa is the second largest continent.

Area: 11.7 million square miles (30.3 million square kilometers)

Population: 807 million

First humans in Africa: 160,000 years ago

First civilizations: Egyptians 5,000 years ago

Other civilizations: Bantu and Zulu tribes, Kingdom of Ghana, Kingdom of Kongo

Countries: 53

Biggest country: Sudan

Smallest country: Seychelles Islands

Most crowded country: Nigeria

Highest point: Kilimanjaro in Tanzania at 19,341 feet (5,895 meters)

Longest river: Nile River in Egypt, Sudan, and Uganda

Climate zones: arid, semiarid, savanna, tropical

African regions: Northern Africa, semiarid Africa, tropical Africa, Southern Africa

Languages: More than 1,500 African languages, as well as Arabic, French, English, and Dutch

Web sites

For more information on Africa go to:
http://www.worldatlas.com/webimage/countrys/af.htm
http://pbskids.org/africa/
http://www.awf.org/

Glossary

apartheid   a system of rule in South Africa that kept black and white people apart

arid   a dry, desert-like climate

barren   having few plants

Christian   a religion that supports the belief in one God and the teachings of Jesus as the son of God

colonized   when one country takes over another country

endangered   at risk of becoming extinct

equator   an imaginary line around the middle of the Earth's surface

ethnic groups   types of people who share similar heritage

extinct   when no more of a particular species of plant or animal are left on the Earth

famine   when people starve because food crops are destroyed by severe drought

highlands   mountainous or hilly country

humid   when there is a large amount of water vapor in the air

hydropower   power made from fast-flowing water

independence   when a country governs itself

Islamic   a religion that believes in one God called Allah and the messages God gave to Muhammed

mammals   animals that feed or suckle their young with milk

Middle East   a group of countries in southwest Asia near Africa including Saudi Arabia, Iran, Iraq, Israel, Lebanon, and Kuwait

nomads   people who move their homes around and do not live in one place for a long time

oasis   a natural water supply in an otherwise dry desert area

pharaoh   a king or queen of ancient Egypt

rain forests   areas dense with tall trees and undergrowth found in hot wet climates

safari   traveling to see wild animals; means "journey" in the Swahili language

savanna   grasslands with scattered trees on the edge of the tropics

segregation   restriction of ethnic groups from certain areas

tectonic plates   large pieces of the Earth's crust that move slowly, causing earthquakes

trading   buying and selling goods

traditions   the way something has been done for many years

tropical   a hot, humid, and wet climate found near the equator

vaccine   medicine that is given to prevent diseases such as polio

Index